Guides of Museu d'Arqueologia de Catalunya

ULLASTRET

Aurora Martín i Ortega

Ullastret
Museu d'Arqueologia
de Catalunya

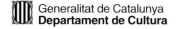

Generalitat de Catalunya
Departament de Cultura

Index

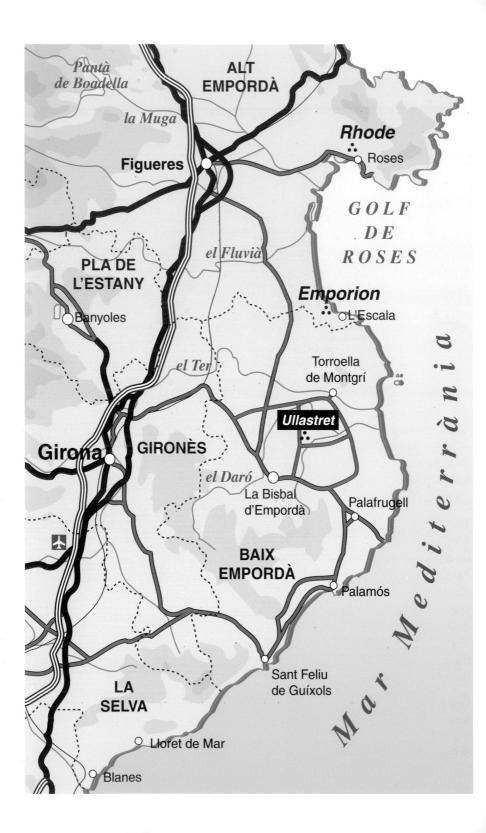

Panoramic view of Puig de Sant Andreu.

Location and access

Ullastret is located in the district of Baix Empordà, six kilometres from the district capital of la Bisbal. It appears on sheet number 296 of the Topographic Map of Spain: scale 1:50,000, and on the Baix Empordà sheet of the Districts Map of Catalonia: scale 1:50,000.

Two important settlements from the Iberian Period have been found in the municipality of Ullastret, these are Puig de Sant Andreu and Illa d'en Reixac, which constitute the present Archaeological Park of Ullastret. Access to the Puig de Sant Andreu site, the only one regularly open to the public, is via a side road leading off the local Ullastret road, approximately 1 kilometre north of the present-day village. This road joins the local Parlavà to Torroella de Montgrí road to the north, and the district road from la Bisbal to Peratallada to the south.

One kilometre north of Puig de Sant Andreu, and only some 400 metres from Illa d'en Reixac, although in the municipality of Serra de Daró, we find the necropolis of Puig de Serra, also from the Iberian Period.

Archaeological research at Ullastret

The first written record of the existence of archaeological remains at Ullastret dates from the year 1931, when Mr. Lluis Pujol i Messeguer, a resident of L'Escala and amateur archaeologist, informed the Associació d'Amics de l'Art Vell of the existence of a pre-Roman settlement at Puig de Sant Andreu. This news was subsequently published by the Association in a Memorandum in 1935, which dealt with the work carried out from 1929 to 1935. The site had, however, been visited by previous studies, at the end of the 19th century J. De Chia having donated Iberian pottery found at Ullastret to the Museu Arqueològic de Girona. There is also evidence that at the beginning of the 20th century blocks of stone from the eastern wall of the settlement were used for building roads, and that when the road that leads to the inside of the old lake through the north of the site was made up, a pottery oven was found otuside the walled site.

As a result of the scientific discovery of the site the Associació d'Amics de l'Art Vell commissioned the archaeologist, Serra Ràfols to identify it. Later Colominas, Pericot and Schulten also visited it.

The Illa d'en Reixac site, seen from Puig de Sant Andreu.

The necropolis of Puig de Serra, with Montgrí in the background.

In 1932, L'Institut d'Estudis Catalans and La Comissió Provincial de Monuments de Girona commissioned the architects Rafael Masó and Josep Gudiol to draw up a preliminary topographical sketch of the Puig de Sant Andreu settlement. This sketch was later published by Serra Ràfols in the 1945-46 edition of the magazine "Empúries", as part of an article about the site.

Despite the interest which had been awoken in the scientific world, excavation work was not started at Ullastret until 1947. The first excavations were supervised by Prof. Pericot, and directed by M. Oliva. After 1952, work was done on an annual basis, financed by the Diputació de Girona, which purchased the Puig de Sant Andreu site between 1954 and 1957. This body also started work on the Museum in 1959, which was inaugurated in 1961.

Since 1959, the investigation work at Ullastret has been programmed and directed by the Servei d'Investigacions Arqueològics, currently the Centre d'Investigacions Arqueològiques del Museu d'Arqueologia de Catalunya-Girona, with the occasional collaboration of the l'Institut d'Arqueologia i Prehistòria de la Universitat de Barcelona.

Until 1974, the investigation work concentrated on Puig de Sant Andreu, however prospective digs were also carried out in the area around the settlement. This resulted in the discovery of various minor settlements which have still not been systematically excavated, with most of the information relating to them resulting from the archaeological materials found on the surface. At the beginning of the sixties, the Illa d'en Reixac site was discovered on a hillock, which in modern times barely stands out above the level of the plain, it is located around 400 metres north-east of the northern tip of Puig de Sant Andreu. This discovery transformed the Iberian sites at Ullastret into a unique discovery, due to the importance and proximity of the two settlements which, individually, are among the most important existing examples of Iberian culture, and Puig, at present, is the largest site in Catalonia. One of the most important questions currently being investigated at Ullastret concerns the nature of the relationship between these two settlements.

Between 1976 and 1995, archaeological research was almost exclusively centred on Illa d'en Reixac, where M. Oliva carried out three excavations between 1965 and 1967. The results of this early work proved to be so important that the Diputació de Girona also acquired this site.

The third of the important sites which make up this group, the necropolis of Puig de Serra, discovered at Serra de Daró in 1982, is the only indigenous necropolis from the Middle Iberian Period to be discovered in this part of Catalonia. Excavation work was done between 1982 and 1986, leading to the discovery of various dispersed Iberian dwellings on the same hilltop site. The land on which this discovery was made is the communal property of the municipality of Serra de Daró.

In 1992 the two settlements and the museum were transferred by the Diputació to the Departament de Cultura de la Generalitat de Catalunya, as a result of the Law Governing Museums, and is currently one of the centres of the Museu d'Arqueologia de Catalunya.

Since 1995, extensive excavation work has been resumed at Puig de Sant Andreu, with the priority of transforming the site into an Archaeological Park. In 1995 and 1996 the museum installations were also renovated.

Environmental context of Ullastret in the Iberian Period

The two settlements at Ullastret and the necropolis of Puig de Serra are located on hills of the Eocene Period, which rise up out of the Quaternary plain of the Baix Empordà, in the very centre of the territory bounded in the north by the Massif of Montgrí, in the west by the Gavarres hills and to the south by the Massif of Begur. They are cut off from the sea to the east by the Sierra de Llavià, less than 20 kilometres away. Other remains from the same period have also been found in the area immediately surrounding these sites, indicating the density of the population of this territory.

Palaeo-climatic studies carried out at Ullastret since 1987, together with the archaeological excavations, have allowed us to discover what the landscape was like in the Iberian Period, considerably different from the way it is today, given that the alluvial sediment deposited by the rivers Daró, and Celsà have filled out the plain, covering over the ancient topography which was considerably more rugged than it is at the present time.

There was a lake between the hills of Puig de Sant Andreu, Puig de Serra to the west, and Serra de Llavià to the east, which was artificially drained after 1885, and which occasionally floods in periods of heavy rainfall. Over the last forty years this has happened on three occasions, in 1959, 1977 and 1994. The lake, of which there are no records after the 14th century, was formed during the lower Holocene Period, between 10,000 and 8,000 years ago, and its size varied over the centuries. In modern times, it measured about 200 hectares and was one of the most important in the Baix

Empordà. Investigations in recent years have demonstrated, as opposed to what was previously believed, that in the Iberian Period it was considerably smaller and the settlements were some distance from the lake shore.

The courses of the rivers were also different from today. The Daró ran between the settlements of Illa d'en Reixac and Puig de Sant Andreu, feeding the lake. Channelling work has been carried out in modern times, which has affected the river courses; only a gully, called the Daró Vell, remains of what was the old water course, running along the foot of Puig de Sant Andreu. Important changes have also been done to the River Ter. In ancient times the main river course ran to the sea to the north of the Massif of Montgrí, close to Empúries, and the branch to the south was secondary, while today the opposite is the case.

Analysis of plant remains found at the sites demonstrates that in the Iberian Period the territory was semi-

The Ullastret lake in 1959.

The Ullastret lake in 1994, with the settlements of Puig and the Illa.

deforested, as a result of cultivation, with land set aside for pasture, as well as the harnessing of the resources of the forests for the construction of dwellings and other uses. The landscape was open, with woods of willow, poplars, elms and tamarisks along the shores of the lake and the river banks, while the higher ground featured vegetation typical of Mediterranean lowlands, with holm, cork and common oak woods, along with white pine and an undergrowth consisting of heather and strawberry tree. In certain areas chestnuts and fir trees were also found.

Analysis of the raw materials used in the manufacture of metal tools and flint implements, of the pottery and the stone blocks employed for building work in the settlements, indicates a good knowledge of the immediate territory and well planned exploitation strategies. The material used for the construction of walls is mostly clay, from Puig de Sant Andreu and Puig de Serra. Other quarries which were exploited were those of Gualta and Clots de San Julià in Peratallada. It has also been possible to demonstrate the selective exploitation of different types of rock, depending on the kind of use it had to serve. Thus mill stones would be made from basalt, which could have been deposited by the rivers, while moulds and mortars were manufactured using sandstone. The metals were manufactured with

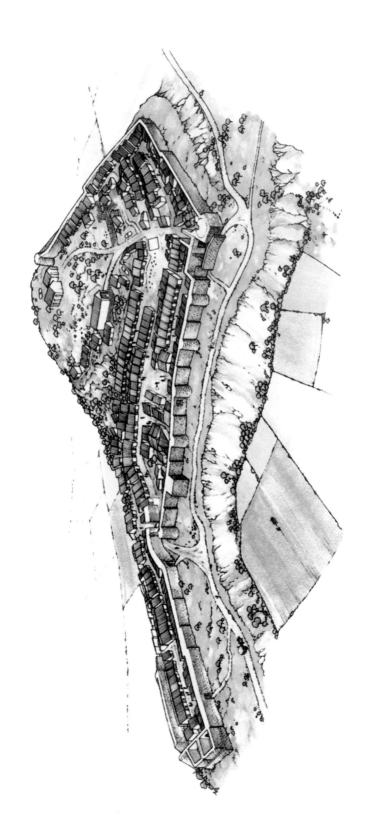

Ideal restoration of the Oppidum of Puig de Sant Andreu.

mineral additives, which came mainly from the neighbouring area of Gavarres, and from the Massif of Begur, but also from the Pyrenees. It was also shown that a considerable number of metal objects were made by recycling useless pieces. Analysis of the clay used in the manufacture of indigenous ceramics and adobe in construction also shows that they originated from the Empordà area.

The Ullastret sites. Historical and archaeological development

The archaeological excavation work done at Puig de Sant Andreu has enabled the documenting of man's presence here since the upper Palaeolithic period, through finds of chipped flint utensils from this age at the level of the bedrock. Neolithic polished stone axes and fragments of bell-shaped type pottery with engraved designs have also been found. The occasional out-of-context finds, also imply sporadic visits by small human groups.

The first important settlements that we know of, found at both Illa d'en Reixac and Puig de Sant Andreu, are from the second half of the 7th century BC, corresponding to the beginning of the Iron Age. The deepest excavations at Illa d'en Reixac have enabled a partial discovery of the first settlement. The dwellings from this period were circular huts, partially carved out of the rock and built up using perishable materials (mud and wood), which were obliterated by subsequent constructions on the same sites. Some remains have, however, been preserved, particularly the holes dug in the ground, into which supports for roofs and cooking hearths were inserted, made out of superimposed layers of pot fragments and clay. In some cases the dwellings have a pit

Lamp of eastern origin, in the form of a sphinx, made of bone.

in the middle, some 50 or 60 cm. deep, carved out of the rock. One of the excavated huts preserved a pre-pared floor of purposely baked and compressed earth, with one of the sides marked off with stones, consti-tuting a rudimentary wall.

This type of settlement has been documented in vari-ous parts of the Empordà area on and near the coast, for example at Sant Martí d'Empúries and Mas Gusó de Bellcaire. At Puig de Sant Andreu the discovery was made after the finding of materials in the south-western area of the settlement, also associated with post holes, although almost completely obliterated by the con-struction of the rampart in the Early Iberian Period. Mate-rials from this age have also been found at Mas Castellar de Pontós, in the villages of Castell de la Fosca de Palamós, Montilivi de Girona and Castell de Porqueres, among others, as many of the Iberian settlements in this area were built on the same sites as dwellings from the early Iron Age.

All of the indigenously produced ceramic vessels found in these huts are hand made, with fluted decorations, the application of raised bands, etc., typical of the late Urnfield Culture. During this period the indigenous pop-ulation of the Empordà came into contact for the first time with the historical Mediterranean civilisations, evi-dence of which is provided by the presence of imported products, particularly ceramics, a testimony to the trading relations established from this period onwards, and which have only been found in small quantities in this early stage. The oldest remains to have been found of this trade are of Phoenician amphorae from the late 7th century B.C. Towards the end of this century, and at the beginning of the 6th century B.C., Etruscan black bucchero-ware amphorae and vases arrived at Ullastret, and Greek materials, particularly those proceeding from the Greek Phocaean colonies in the Gulf of Lyon, from *Massilia* (modern Marseilles), and *Emporion* (modern Empúries), founded about 600 BC.

Contact between the native population and these more advanced cultures led to the development of the Iberian Culture over an extensive area stretching from Languedoc to Andalusia, represented by a variety of regional aspects. In the Empordà area, occupied by a tribe, identified in ancient sources as the Indiketa, the presence of the Greek colony of *Emporion* was to have an important repercussion on the subsequent development of Iberian Culture, which was also culturally influenced by neighbouring Southern Gallia, as well as by the Phoenician-Carthaginian world.

Iberian Culture at Ullastret, as was the case in the indigenous world in north-eastern Catalonia in general, came into being around 550 BC. Initially, in what is known as the Early Iberian Period, the first houses based on a rectangular ground plan were built, having walls built with adobe on stone plinths, the upper parts of which generally have not survived. The houses had flattened earth floors, prepared for drainage. In some cases the remains of dividing walls within the houses have been found; these were exclusively adobe, without a stone plinth. This type of construction first appears in this area of Catalonia during the Early Iberian Period, although in other parts of the country this kind of solid construction dates back to earlier times. The central pit is a feature dating from the Middle to Late Bronze Age, and in the lower Ebro valley since the second half of the 7th century BC.

Etruscan amphora. Middle of the 6th century.

General view of the west rampart, showing the polygonal towers.

The archaeological artifacts found in these first settlements of the Iberian Period show, as with the architecture, the adoption by the indigenous population of new techniques copied from the colonists. Most of the pottery manufactured from this time onwards was made using the fast potter's wheel, and hand-made pottery became limited to cooking utensils, due to its greater plasticity and resistance to fire. Early indigenous production was centred on painted Iberian pottery which can be found throughout the Iberian world of this period. In the same workshops, imitations were also made of the monochrome grey ceramics manufactured by the Phocaean Greeks at the colonies in the Gulf of Lyon. These locally manufactured products are often found accompanied by materials originating from trade with the Mediterranean world, in which *Emporion* would have acted as the intermediary. Most of the amphorae which arrived during this period are of Greco-Phoenician origins, as was the case throughout the whole of the Iberian Period, both at Ullastret and in other settlements, demonstrating the importance of trading relations between *Emporion* and the Carthaginian world. Materials were also found, particularly pottery, from the western Greek colonies, and after 535 BC luxury dishes began to arrive from Athens, sometimes with black-figure decoration and sometimes undecorated.

Fragment of a *kratera* with red figures, featuring a banquet scene by the Marlay painter, around 430 BC.

Towards the end of the 6th century, the first fortifications were built at Puig de Sant Andreu. The preparation of the land for this building work obliterated a whole section of the walls of the oldest rectangular ground plan dwellings. The rampart was defended by circular towers unique in the Iberian world of Catalonia, with the exception of the tower in the settlement at Mas Castellar de Pontós, which was also in Indiketa territory. The rampart enclosed a settlement which was at most 400 metres in length, running North to South.

At Illa d'en Reixac, although the excavation work has not been as thorough, the remains of early Iberian constructions have been periodically discovered in all of the exploratory digs at the top of the hill and along the eastern and southern slopes. An impressive rampart built along a natural break in the level of the ground has also been interpreted as a rampart from this period. The quantity of these remains that have been found at the site reveal the importance of Iberian occupation from the earliest period of this culture.

The exploratory digs carried out at Puig de Serra, between 1982 and 1986, demonstrated that this hill was also occupied during the Early Iberian Period, although the level of occupation was not very significant, featuring basic dwellings, similar to the pre-Iberian huts, with structures supported by posts, lacking stone walls, but

Kylix with red figures. Last quarter of the 5th century.

with thrown pottery. It is possible that these dwellings were related to activities of community surveillance, as a wide stretch of territory to the north and the east can be observed from Puig de Serra. They may also have been related to work at the quarry where stone was cut from the side of the hill, and where most of the stone used in the construction of Illa d'en Reixac and part of that used for Puig de Sant Andreu was extracted.

Relations with the colonial Mediterranean world intensified during the second half of the 6th century BC and the first half of the following, as demonstrated by the growing presence of imported ceramics. After the middle of the 5th century BC at the beginning of the Middle Iberian Period, Attic Greek ceramics were introduced in ever increasing quantities, distributed among all of the Iberian settlements in Catalonia from the last quarter of this century until around 350 BC. Alongside these can be found products of diverse origins from the central and western Mediterranean, resulting from trade based on bartering, in which the indigenous population offered cereals and raw materials in exchange for manufactured products, particularly ceramics, as well as amphorae containing olive oil and wine which, as stated above, came mainly from the Carthaginian world.

From the second half of the 5th century onwards a material culture developed in the Indiketa area of the Iberian world with features which are mainly attributable to the Hellenization of the territory. The efforts of the indigenous population to imitate Greek ceramics is evident, leading to the gradual abandonment of the Iberian painted ceramic production of the previous period, substituted by the production of thin walled jars made from dark coloured clays, with white paint applied after the pottery had been fired. The decorative friezes in most cases copied Attic pottery, in the *Saint-Valentin* style. This style of ceramics was developed at Ullastret as well as in other settlements in the Indiketa area, such as Sant Julià de Ramis, and was basically distributed over an area stretching from Tordera to L'Albera, although it can be found as far afield as L'Erau in the north, and in the south appears in various settlements of the *Layetana*. In Ullastret, from the beginning of the 4th century onwards, the shapes of the Attic vases, which began to arrive on the market place at that time, were also imitated by the production of table ware denominated, Catalan coastal ware.

Between 400 and 350 BC important rebuilding work was carried out on the ramparts of the two Ullastret settlements. At the *Oppidum*, or walled town, of Puig de Sant Andreu, the ramparts were almost completely rebuilt, with extensions which almost doubled the size of the enclosed space. The excavation work done between 1991 and 1993, at the southern end of the Illa settlement

Puig Sant Andreu. Seen from the temple area, with tower no. 7.

Western rampart of Puig de Sant Andreu.

revealed a rampart with similar constructive characteristics to the one at Puig, dating from the first half of the 4th century BC. Most of the graves which have survived from the Puig de Serra necropolis are also from this same period.

From the end of the 4th century BC, Italic products increasingly began to appear, evidence of the introduction into this area of the north-eastern Mediterranean of the new dynamic of relations between Mediterranean peoples which preceded the Punic Wars.

The archaeological remains of the later stages of these two settlements demonstrate the consolidated scale of the occupation of Ullastret during the 3rd century BC, corresponding to the time of the construction of various public and/or religious buildings in both settlements. The recent excavation of levels corresponding to this stage at the site of Illa d'en Reixac, has provided a great deal of information about aspects which previously were very little known, such as spiritual life and beliefs, providing evidence of ritual similarities with the indigenous world of southern Gallia, side by side with those taken from the Carthaginian world. In the 3rd century BC, a new stage of rebuilding work on the ramparts of Puig de Sant Andreu was also undertaken, probably related to the Second Punic War, as was also the case at Empúries.

In 218 BC, during the war, the Romans disembarked at Empúries which resulted in a rapid decline of the indigenous way of life in the Empordà area. At Ullastret, the Catonian repression of 195 BC led to the disappearance of the two settlements as independent indigenous communities, although a residual occupation may have continued, perhaps in connection with the continuity of the temple cult at the top of the hill. Excavations have unearthed ceramic materials from the first half of the 2nd century BC, as well as Roman coins from the time of both the High and Low Empire. There are also remains of a Late Roman necropolis on the southern slope of Puig, found during the first excavations in 1947.

In the Mediaeval period a castle was built at Puig de Sant Andreu, with a moat, ramparts and towers, which is still standing in part and has been identified with the one at *Vellosos*, which was documented in the 9th century. The castle at Puig was abandoned after the building of the fortified town of present day Ullastret, in the 11th and 12th centuries. In the 16th century the hermitage of San Andreu was built in the popular Gothic style, taking partial advantage of the castle walls; a farm house was later built on the same site. The remains from these building were used in the construction of the museum in modern times.

At the end of the 17th century, and in connection with the first attempts to drain the Ullastret lake, large scale earth movements were made at both Illa d'en Reixac and Puig de Sant Andreu to re-condition the land, preparing it for cultivation, which involved the building of terraces on the Puig hill, the removal of the top and the filling out of the lower perimeter area of the Illa. These large scale earth movements resulted in significant damage to the sites, particularly at the levels corresponding to the later stages of the Iberian settlement, which has disappeared over extensive areas, particularly at the Illa. This in turn has led to erroneous interpretations of these later stages which the current programme of excavations has been able to correct.

Puig de Sant Andreu

The *oppidum* of Puig de Sant Andreu is located on a hill, almost triangular in shape, with one vertex of the rampart facing north and the other two facing south-east and south-west respectively. It is some 600 metres long, on a north-south axis, with a maximum width of 380 metres, east to west. The maximum height is 54 metres above sea level and about 30 metres above the level of the surrounding land. The pronounced variation in the level of the land is particularly reflected on the southern side, which features steep slopes running down to the plain, while the west side offers a more gentle profile, due to the orography as well as the adaptation of the subsoil for human occupation during prehistoric times.

The archaeological excavations have been mainly carried out along the western and southern flanks of the site; however exploratory digs on the eastern side have confirmed that from the 4th century BC onwards, the settlement occupied almost the whole of the hill, and was fortified on all sides.

The steepness of the slope on which the settlement was founded provides the principal reason for the structure of the urban layout which was organised, in most cases, on the basis of long parallel streets, following the curve of the hill. Thick walls have also been discovered along the west slope, up to 2 metres high, which were built along the fault lines of sharp drops in the level of the slope, forming terraced surfaces on which dwellings were built. 209 silos were also found on this slope, carved out of the rock for grain storage. Some of these are within the ramparts, while others are found outside the limits of the settlement.

Recommended route for visitors

Access to the site and the museum is from the west side of Puig de Sant Andreu. It is recommended that the visit should be started outside the settlement, following the

Gate no. 1 in the ramparts of Puig de Sant Andreu.

length of the rampart, from its northern end, and entering through gate 1.

The rampart

The rampart is the largest and most completely preserved indigenous fortification of the Iberian Period in Catalonia. As has been explained above, it was built in various stages, the most important of which are; the first, in the Early Iberian Period; the major rebuilding and extension in the middle of the 6th century BC, and the further extension work which was carried out in around 400 BC, in the Middle Iberian Period. Up to now some 830 metres have been unearthed, closing off the southern, eastern, and part of the western flanks.

Significant remains of the first rampart, enclosing a triangular space, are still standing along the western side, from the south-western corner as far as gate 4 located at the northern end of the earliest enclosure. The first part of this section of the rampart has recently been unearthed, flanking the settlement along its eastern side.

Six truncated cone-shaped towers, along the western flank are also known from this first fortification. Although the construction of these towers is not directly built into the adjacent sections of the rampart they were undoubtedly erected at the same time, with the

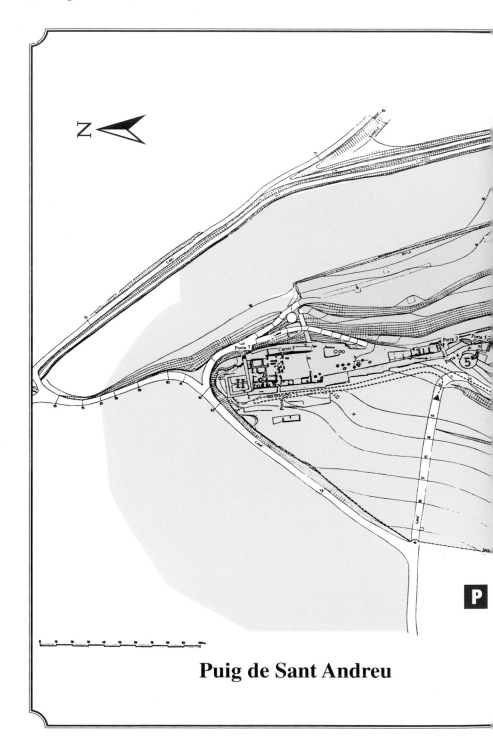

Puig de Sant Andreu

The square tower on the western rampart.

towers being built first and later the sections of the rampart which link them. There are five towers between gates 1 and 4, with the sixth to the south of gate 1. The towers are equidistant from each other, some 28 or 29 metres apart; this implies that the square tower, found between numbers 4 and 5, was built over the site of an earlier tower which must have been destroyed some time during the Middle Iberian Period. Access to the top of the ramparts was by way of spiral staircases inside the towers, remains of which are still evident in towers 5 and 6. At the top of Puig there is a seventh tower, with a circular ground plan, which was incorporated into the Mediaeval castle.

The ramparts built during the middle Iberian Period used the older fortifications as a foundation for the section which runs from the south-western corner as far as gate 4, from which point onwards the settlement was extended. The inside of the rampart was used as a banquette, with the outer side being extensively refaced. At this stage the rampart was adapted to the perimeter of the hill along the eastern and western sides, enclosing a quarry in the north-eastern part of Puig, which had been worked during the previous period. Along the southern side, despite the bad state in which the rampart was found, due in part to the steep slopes on which it was built, three distinct sections can be seen. The section which lies between the south-western corner and tower 7 maintains the same formal characteristics as the rest of the construction and probably follows the line of the older fortifications, while the section after this tower is much narrower, running down from the highest part of the hill to join up with a gate halfway down the slope.

The outer face of the rampart features recesses, the purpose of which is unknown, but which are also found along the south rampart of the Illa d'en Reixac site, built at the time of the extension of the Puig rampart. Along the excavated sections three main gates have been found up to now, with four posterns, or secondary gates. Gates 1 and 4 face west from the settlement, with gate 6 to the south, all three have an entrance passage which increased the defensive capabilities of the accesses to the interior of the settlement. Gates 1 and 4 are flanked by towers, gate 1 also has an advanced defensive system of which some walls in front of the gate are still standing. Three of the posterns are located between gate 4 and the north-eastern corner of Puig, with the fourth at the north-eastern corner itself, at the foot of the north tower access stairway.

The fortifications of the Middle Iberian Period make use of the polygonal towers of the old rampart. The access system to the top of the rampart was modified, in this

View of the inside of the settlement.

new stage by means of stairs which run perpendicular to the line of the ramparts and towers. The continual building of dwellings which backed onto the inside of the rampart resulted in a constant raising of the ground level, as a result of which these stairways end far above the level of the bases of the towers.

Subsequent to this stage of extensions further reforms were occasionally incorporated into the defensive system of the *oppidum*. One of these was the rebuilding of gate 1 and the immediate area, as it is presently found, as well as that of the square tower on the western flank, characterised by the fact that a recess, or slot, runs along the length of the rampart, the purpose of which is unknown, and which has also been found on the ramparts of other Indiketa Iberian settlements, at Castell de la Fosca in Palamós and at Creueta near Girona. Another modification was the construction of the north tower, the largest of the towers, with sides measuring 15 metres. This tower was built on the site of the quarry on the northern flank of the settlement, built into the northern face of the rampart and with its walls stepped to provide greater solidity.

Between towers 1 and 2 there was a rainwater drainage channel, traversing the width of the wall. It is possible that there were others but the bad condition of large sections of the rampart do not allow this to be confirmed with any certainty.

Some of the gates, among them No. 1, when they were discovered, were found blocked off. This and the slipshod nature of the lining of tower No. 6, adjacent to the gate, seems to indicate that there may have been a siege, possibly related to the end of the life of the settlement, under adverse conditions in a confrontation with the Romans.

The interior of the settlement

Entering by the gateway at the end of the access passage we find street No. 1, running perpendicular to the slope of the hill of Puig de Sant Andreu. Only the first 40 metres of this street, which must have run between the gate and the top part of the settlement, are known, after which point it would have continued through a sector of the site which was completely demolished during the excavations carried out for the laying of the access road leading up to the museum, which follows a random path. Three streets lead off perpendicularly from either sides of this first street, two towards the south, denominated A and B, and one towards the north, street C. These streets follow the contours of the hillside.

Immediately after the access passage to gate 1, before the start of street A, we find the entrance to tower 6. At current street level we can observe the old interior stairway, and at an elevation of 1 metre, built into the wall of the tower itself, the exterior stairway from the middle Iberian Period.

Street A leads to the south-western end of the settlement. Between the street and the wall we find the so-called south-eastern quarter. In this area remains have been conserved of all the different construction stages of the settlement, from the earliest occupation, in pre-Iberian times, to the period when it was finally abandoned. The result is, as can be seen, a continuous superimposition of walls, generally of limited elevation, which are the remains of the base levels of the various dwellings from different constructive periods. At the southern end of the street we can clearly see a wall from the middle Iberian Period built on top of an older wall using the latter as a foundation, there are also walls dating back to before the original rampart, and which have been cut off by it. In this street we also find silos cut into the base rock.

From the end of street A we can see the south-western corner of the Puig rampart, and further on an open area next to the rampart, around which several dwellings were laid out with colonnaded antechambers. In two of these the sandstone column plinths which supported the corresponding colonnade are still standing. It was assumed that this group of buildings might well have been a square, or *agora*, when it was first discovered, however it is now believed that this was a complex building, probably serving a public purpose, and laid out around a large patio. This new interpretation has been arrived at due to its similarity to another large building of similar characteristics unearthed in recent years at the Illa d'en Reixac site. The quality of the building work, and the elevation of the stone plinths of the walls also indicate the character of a public work. Chronologically it dates back to the second half of the 3rd century BC, corresponding to the last construction stage of the settlement.

In the patio, below the level of this great building we can see the remains of earlier walls, some of which have been cut off by the rampart, and in the bedrock there are more silos. Further on, along the same side of the street, there are a number of dwellings with one or two rooms.

Street B, parallel to street A, has its stone paving partially conserved and ends in a group of dwellings which back onto the southern rampart. One of the settlement's cisterns is located between this street and the large public building described above, built in the 3rd century BC and imitating the design of the cisterns at Empúries. These cisterns were used for the storage of the population's supply of drinking water, which was collected from the roofs when it rained. As well as this cistern in street B, there is another next to the roadway which leads up to the museum (along the recommended return route), and a third, the largest, underneath the museum itself, with a capacity of 130,000 litres.

All three of these cisterns are oval in shape, were carved out of the bedrock and were lined with extremely regular sandstone ashlars, with a roughcast of limestone mortar, which has partially survived to the present day. The cistern in street B has provided a great deal of information as to how these functioned, as it was discovered partially covered over with large stone slabs, on one of which we can see fittings for the protection system at the mouth of the cistern, from which water was taken. On one side there is a lead gutter, for channelling water, and at the other an opening, allowing for the overflow of excess water. Two cisterns of the same type were found at the Castell de Fosca settlement, in Palamós.

Before the introduction of these kinds of cisterns, the drinking water was stored in deposits carved out of the bedrock. It is probable that a rectangular deposit found in this same street, at the junction with street 1, served this purpose.

From street B, access via a modern stairway can be gained to the continuation of the area of the dwellings which back onto the rampart, continuing to the top levels of the site.

Gate no. 2 in the wall of the *oppidum.*

The buildings which can be seen in this area are the remains of dwellings, with the simple floor plans described above, and generally speaking with one or two rooms. Although stairs have been found in both of the settlements the houses, generally speaking, only consisted of a ground floor. The construction system, discussed above, was based on walls with stone plinths, held together with mud mortar, and with adobe elevations, although at the Illa none have been found on-site so far. The walls must have been dressed with a mud lining, particularly on the outside, in order to make them impermeable. Occasional remains of this lining have been found, and the insides of the houses show occasional signs of having been painted.

The roofing was supported on wooden rafters, resting on the tops of the perimeter walls, and occasionally inside the dwellings certain elements have been found, such as stone slabs, or holes in the ground, which imply the existence of wooden uprights which would have held up the main beam. In the first case, the roofing would only have had one slope, in the second there might have been two slopes. On top of the rafters a layer of twigs and branches would have been placed, finally dressed with a layer of mud to render it impermeable.

All of the houses had a fire-place, used for cooking and heating. Fire-places were built throughout the Iberian Period in the same way as they were built in the pre-Iberian, laid out on the floor of the house, or in small depressions dug into the floor, with ceramic or small clay stone bottoms. The smoke escaped through a hole in the roof. In some

Street B, with stone paving and the cistern.

house plinths for domestic ovens have also been found, such as in a small room, open to the street in the north of the site, next to postern gate 2, which suggest that some of them must have had a community function, as was also the case in the settlement of Puig Castellet in Lloret de Mar. They must surely have been used for baking bread. Some of the houses also had benches, made of stone or adobe and built into one of the walls, which may have been either for sitting on or for tableware. The floors of the houses were normally of beaten earth, although some of the public buildings, towards the end of the life of the settlement, had *opus signinum* paved floors. Some of the patios have also been found paved with flat stones or river pebbles.

At the top of the site there is a sacred area in which two temples have been discovered, of the *in antis* type, as well as the largest of the cisterns. The two temples faced east, with the one to the south being smaller and in a better state of conservation, it was built on a rectangular floor plan, and only a part of the northern wall of the entrance hallway survives, this is a result of the building of the castle which destroyed this sector of the building. The interior room still preserves remains of the *opus signinum* paving, decorated with white marble mosaic tiles. It had exterior abutments, of which three remain on the northern side, and two to the south and the east. Worshippers at this temple used to bring numerous earthenware *ex votive* offerings, featuring the moulded faces of Gorgons and other mythological figures which would have been coloured, although no trace of the paint has been preserved.

Next to this temple, and laid out in line with it, we find the southern wall of the other temple building with a similar, but larger, ground plan. Part of the northern wall is also still standing, and runs under the custodian's house, as well as the wall which separated the two rooms. The southern wall was lined with coarse stucco of a reddish colour. The layout of the sacred quarter, occupying the top part of the hill, is an imitation of the style of many Greek cities, and for this reason in an attempt at assimilation, this area has, in modern times, been referred to as the *acropolis*.

It is possible that on this top level of Puig there were other buildings, which have been destroyed by building work in both Mediaeval and modern times. A mosaic of black and white tiles, which do not come from either of the temples, appears to be from this area, and could belong to a religious building from a period after the site had been abandoned as a settlement.

The museum installations and the remains of the towers of the Medieval castle, one of which was built on top of the Iberian fortifications, tower 7, can also be found in this area. An observation point has been installed on the foundations of another Mediaeval tower, overlooking the plain.

Having arrived at this point, it is a good moment to visit the museum, which is described in the following chapter.

Behind the museum there is another observation point from which the settlement of Illa d'en Reixac can be seen to the north-west, between Puig de Sant Andreu and the Llavià hills, and to the north Puig de Serra, where the necropolis was found.

Going down towards Street 1, on the right side of the road there is a quarter in which we can see, among others, a building with an elongated floor plan, including a large interior room, some 11 metres long and 5 metres wide,

Interior view of the settlement.

with an antechamber which was probably also colonnaded, as column plinths have been found at both sides of the doorway. The use of this building is uncertain, although it has been suggested that it may have been another temple.

Continuing a little further along this main road we come across another of the cisterns. A study of the several superimposed layers of mortar lining shows us that it was relined on various occasions. During excavation work, the rim of a well, which is now on display in the museum, was unearthed beside the cistern and which must have been installed on the cistern's covering stone slabs.

At the start of street C, where this converges with street 1, there is a large rectangular cavity carved out of the rock which also appears to have been used as a water deposit. On the same side of the street a group of silos can also be seen, while on the other side there is an area of dwellings located between the street and the rampart. The floors of some of the rooms are bedrock, which further on drops away sharply. This can be clearly seen to the north of the rampart, marking off one of the great terracing walls which were described when explaining the urban implantation system of the settlement. Traversing this wall, at the bottom, street D runs parallel to the rampart.

From this point we are offered a panoramic view of the fortifications from the inside, from gate 1 to tower 2. In the angle of the rampart and tower 1 we can identify three periods in the construction of the wall facings. There is also a certain discontinuity in the walls of the tower, which leads us to believe that this section had been restored.

The remains of stairs, which were built into the tower, can also be seen, possibly dating from two different periods.

Between street D and the rampart there is a group of dwellings, stretching as far as tower 2. We can also see the drainage outlet on the inside. Built into the wall, where this is joined to the tower, there is the longest of the remaining exterior stairways. The part of the site which is open to visitors ends here.

At the present time work is going ahead on excavations in the area between gate 4 and tower 4. This work has allowed us to discover the layout of street 2, which leads up from this gateway, and which possibly converges with street C. If this is confirmed it would represent the most important street in the settlement. It was paved at various stages, with pebbles and flags. Inside the entrance passage of gate 4 there is a water drainage channel, which presumably ran underneath the wooden top covering the opening.

Between street 2 and the rampart various dwelling areas have been discovered, corresponding to the later stages of the life of the settlement, with archaeological materials which permit the dating of their abandonment to the beginning of the 2nd century BC. From earlier excavation work in this area we also know of some houses from an earlier period, which were burnt down in a fire at the beginning of the 4th century BC. Due to their size, and the wealth of archaeological materials found there, with imported ceramics particularly abundant, they must have belonged to aristocratic families.

To the north of gate 4, the site has been less well studied, except for the most northerly end of the settlement, where a street, F, was found, which skirted the eastern rampart from gate 7, and was about 4 metres wide. The including of the quarry within the *oppidum*, exploited during the Early Iberian Period for the building of houses, meant that some of the houses in this area used the steps, produced in the bedrock by the extraction of stone blocks, as a back wall.

Illa d'en Reixac

The settlement at Illa is located some 400 metres north-east of Puig de Sant Andreu, on a rectangular shaped hillock with a length of about 320 metres running north to south, and a width of some 200 metres east to west. It rises to a height of 13 metres above sea level. The excavation work done on this site has still not allowed the full extent of the settlement to be determined, although it appears to have covered an area of over 5 hectares. It is called the Illa because in modern times it was a small island on the lake, close to the western shore, although we now know that this was not the case in ancient times.

The chronology and material culture of the site are the same as at Puig. The exploratory digs carried out at the end of the seventies were fundamental in establishing the sequence of the Iberian world in north-eastern Catalonia, from the earliest period until Romanization, and for reaching an understanding about pre-Iberian occupation at Ullastret. The extensive excavations of recent years have shown that an extended area at the top of the hill was destroyed at the end of the 17th century or the beginning of the 18th, when the land was turned over to cultivation. This resulted in the disappearance of the most recent levels, with the result that for some time it was believed

Illa d'en Reixac.

that the site had been abandoned at the beginning of the 4th century BC. Although on the lower slopes of the hill the later stages of life at this site have been well preserved, and it has been possible to excavate structures from this period, among which is a large building serving a ritual purpose, with an area of 1,000 m².

The Illa settlement was fortified, along the southern side of the hill the remains of a rampart built at the beginning of the 4th century BC have been found. At the present time a section, some 30 metres in length, has been unearthed, with a width of some 3 metres and a height, still standing, of almost 4 metres. The lower part of this rampart is found at phreatic levels, a fact which introduces many problems in terms of study and conservation. The first excavation work to be done at the site led to the discovery of a great wall at the bottom of the slope of the hill, which was interpreted by the then site archaeologist, M. Oliva, as an Early Iberian rampart, an interpretation which has yet to be confirmed. It can, however, be confirmed that an Early Iberian fortification existed at the Illa, which was later extended or restored in the Middle Iberian Period.

The urban plan is more regular than that at Puig, presenting an orthogonal layout. This is due to the much gentler and more even slopes of the hill.

This site is currently under excavation and is not generally open to the public.

Detail view of an exploratory dig on the rampart of Illa d'en Reixac.

Puig de Serra

This site is found approximately 1 Km. north of Puig de Sant Andreu, and some 700 metres from Illa d'en Reixac. On this hillock the remains of Early Iberian occupation have been unearthed and also the necropolis from the Middle Iberian Period. It has also been possible to doc-

Burial offerings and urn from Puig de Serra. First half of the 4th century BC.

ument the use of the quarry for the extraction of construction materials for both of the settlements during the Iberian Period.

The location of the site on a terrain which has been continually used for the extraction of soil and as a quarry for public works in the municipality of Serra de Daró has meant that the necropolis is in a very degraded state, and it is impossible to discover what its full size might have been.

The fact that the graves were not covered with any kind of stone tumulus to protect them, has added to this advanced state of deterioration. There are various types of grave, although the most common consists of holes dug in the surface soil to the depth of the bedrock, with a cavity carved into the rock itself, in which a cinerary urn was deposited, sometimes accompanied by funeral goods. A total of sixty such graves have been discovered in varying degrees of preservation, with most dating from the end of the 5th century BC and the beginnings of the 4th century BC, yet there are none from the first half of the 5th or the 3rd centuries BC. This has led us to believe that the site must have been much larger. This hypothesis is also supported by the fact that an enormous quantity of highly fragmented, contextual material has been found, which must have come from graves which have been destroyed.

The museum

The museum is situated at the top of the hill. It was built on the site of the hermitage dedicated to the patron saint of Ullastret, Sant Andreu (*Saint Andrew*), whose name was given to this hill *(Puig)*. The building is in the popular Gothic style and has been recently restored. Remains of the medieval castle, which was also located at *Puig*, can also be seen, of which, in the present building, a good part of the north wall and the bases of the three towers have been preserved. The first room of the museum was inaugurated in 1961, with the later addition of two more rooms. The museum is concerned with Iberian culture in the northeast of Catalonia, based on the results of the excavations on the sites found at Ullastret.

In Room 1 the sites are represented from a chronological and palaeo-climatic point of view, defining the characteristics of Iberian culture and explaining the periodic distribution established for the study. There are also explanations of the district, coinage and spiritual life, beliefs and funerary rights. In room 2, urbanism. In room 3, the language and writing of the Iberian Period, along with economic and productive activities, agriculture and stock-breeding, and crafts. Each of these themes is described on one or more panels, with texts and illustrations, accompanied by display cases exhibiting the archaeological materials discussed. The panels explaining the time-scale are accompanied by display cases exhibiting an extensive range of materials characteristic of each stage of the Iberian culture. The colouring of the background of the panels is also different, reflecting their contents, either general (ochre) or specific (mauve).

Room 1

Chronology

Iberian culture is placed within the chronological-cultural sequence of human history, from the lower Palaeolithic Period until the present, as well as the testimonies of other ages, both previous and subsequent, found in the excavations of the Ullastret sites.

The chronology is complemented by the exhibition of archaeological materials from each of the different periods: flint utensils from the Upper Palaeolithic Period and Campanian ceramic pot shards from the Chalcolithic Period, found at *Puig de Sant Andreu*; ceramics from the early Iron Age, from *Puig* and from the *Illa*, a painted Iberian ceramic vase and Roman coins found at *Puig*. Modern times are represented by two photographs of the first excavations at *Puig de Sant Andreu*, at the end of the forties.

The geology-geography-landscape of Ullastret in the Iberian Period

As has been explained in the chapter concerning the environmental context, studies of the palaeo-climatic conditions carried out over recent years, along with the excavation work, show that the scenery and vegetation of the Iberian Period differed considerably from those of the present day. On this panel an explanation is given of their characteristics, and all that is known about the extent of the lake which was, in ancient times, much smaller than had been supposed in comparison with its size in the Mediaeval and modern periods. This information is accompanied by a geomorphological map of the lake, photographs of the floods of 1959 and 1994, and representations of the flora and fauna of the Iberian Period. Information is also included about the drainage of the lake, which was begun in 1856, and completed some thirty years later.

The forming of Iberian culture. Iberian culture and society

Panels three and four synthesise all that is explained in the rest of the museum, as well as summarising some of the chapters of this guide, and thus we will only make a passing reference to them. The most characteristic features of Iberian culture are defined: an economy based on agriculture and stock-breeding; the development of the urban phenomenon, iron metal working and the adoption of the fast potter's wheel for the manufacture of ceramics; the intensification of trade and bartering, with the appearance of coinage towards the end of the period; the general practice of cremation as a funerary rite; the appearance of the first indigenous writing system; the existence of a structured society with social classes and division of labour. Two maps are also included, one showing the Iberian tribes which occupied the territory, ranging from Andalusia to Western Languedoc, and the other of the north-western Mediterranean coast, indicating the most important contemporary sites, from Marseilles to the river Ebro.

This section is accompanied by a model of the area Ullastret-Serra de Daró, featuring the settlements of Puig de Sant Andreu and Illa d'en Reixac; the necropolis at Puig de Serra; the old Empúries road, at the northern end of which a small Roman bridge still stands; Daró Vell, which is now a dry gully, but which was once the main course of the river which ran down from les Gavarres, before its course was redirected and channelled; and finally the current maximum limits reached by the lake on its occasional reappearances.

Next, there is a presentation of the Iberian Period in Catalonia. The information on each of the different periods includes:

A map of the Iberian Indiketa territory, with the documented sites from this period, colour coded according to their type: settlements, colonies, necropolises, silo fields. The extension of the occupation of the territory throughout this period can be clearly seen.

A map of the Ullastret-Serra de Daró area, with the representation of the main sites which existed during the period.

A list of the most representative locally manufactured and imported ceramics.

Pre-Iberian Period: 650-550 BC

This was a period in Catalonia which was witness to the economic and social evolution of the late Bronze Age to that of the Iron Age. The arrival of the historical Mediterranean cultures in the area, in the second half of the 7th century BC resulted in the intensification of the use of iron, which had already been introduced by the Indo-Europeans, although it had continued to be an exotic product. The panel shows a photograph of the *Camallera* antenna sword (Alt Empordà), one of the oldest iron products to have been found in Catalonia. A map also shows the main Greek and Phoenician colonies in the central and western Mediterranean. Empúries, on the coast of the Alt Empordà was the most westerly of the colonies established by the Phocaean Greeks along the north-western arc of the Mediterranean, possibly being founded from Marseilles. The native settlements in the Empordà in this period consisted of huts with a circular floor plan, such as those found at Illa d'en Reixac, of which we are offered a speculative reconstruction, as well as the reconstruction of a hut from the Fonollera site, at Torroella de Montgrí, from the late Bronze Age.

The indigenous ceramics from this period were exclusively hand made, offering a great variety of shapes and decorative motifs, indicating their use for a wide range of functions, cooking, storage, table ware, etc. In the Iberian Period, with the spreading of the use of the potter's wheel these products became stereotyped. In the display case you can see fragments of various pieces with the decorations and finishes which were typical of the pre-Iberian Period: grooves, ribs applied to the surface, impressions, incisions, combing, burnishing, markings made with spatulas, bevelled rims, etc. In the display case featuring imports we have Phoenician, Etruscan and Greek materials. Phoenician amphorae began to arrive towards the end of the 7th century BC. It also appears evident that there were Etruscan merchants in the Empordà area, who introduced amphorae and *kantharos* (cups) of the kind known as

Etrusco-Corinthian vase. Middle of the 6th century.

bucchero nero during the first half of the 6th century BC, which is also the period in which the first Greek objects were introduced, originating from eastern Greece, or possibly copies of this style made in the Phocaean colonies, particularly Ionic cups. A fragment of a Corinthian *aryballos* has also been found at Illa, and an Etruscan-Corinthian zoomorphic vase, found on the bedrock of the south-western area of Puig, together with an Ionic *olpes*, a *kantharos* and an Etruscan amphora.

The Early Iberian Period: 550-450 BC

The adoption of the technological developments of the colonial cultures by the indigenous population resulted in an authentic renovation of the economy and in their way of life. Settlements started to be established on fortified hill sites, although, as in the previous period, some also continued to occupy the plains.

The most important developments are illustrated on this panel: a floor plan, the wall and roof of a house illustrate the new building system adopted, with a square ground plan and stone walls, a fast potter's wheel for the manufacture of ceramics, the use of which transformed the production of pottery, which during the previous period must have been mainly for domestic use, and subsequently was to become an organised craft activity; and a metal-working oven. At Illa d'en Reixac iron reduction slag has been found, at the level corresponding to the end of the 6th century BC, confirming the first manufacture of this metal at Ullastret. On the panel you can also see a photograph of tower 5, with its interior spiral staircase.

The indigenous materials exhibited include hand made ceramics, still numerous in this period, and early ceramics manufactured with the potter's wheel, which are of two types: Iberian painted and grey monochrome. Ceramics manufacture using the potter's wheel in the indigenous world of the Empordà started as early as 550 BC, copying the styles which were introduced from

Grey monochrome and Western grey ceramic plate 525-475 BC.

Monochrome grey ceramic jar, 525-450 BC.

Fragments of a Greek vase with black figures, from Illa d'en Reixac, 490-480 BC.

other cultures. The painted Iberian variety was more influenced by ceramics from the south-east of the peninsula. These pieces are mostly storage jars, biconical or oval in shape, and decorated with wine coloured or brown paintings featuring geometric motifs, lines and horizontal parallel stripes, concentric circles and semicircles, tails, etc. which on occasions covered almost the whole surface of the vase. Sometimes these colours were combined with white to form chessboard or dog's tooth motifs, among others. It is possible that the production of monochrome grey ceramics began around the same time, imitating those of the Phocaean Greeks from Marseilles or Empúries. The shapes of these grey pots are sometimes copies of Greek ones, while others reproduce traditional, hand-made forms from the previous period. There are also biconical and oval storage jars, although most of the pieces which have been unearthed are tableware. It has been demonstrated that both of these different pottery types were produced in the same workshops, and using the same clays.

Other indigenously manufactured objects on exhibition include two bronze belt buckles, with three hooks, one of which still has the pin, and a silver decoration in the plate and heel of the piece, as well as various arrowheads also made in bronze.

The imported ceramics are much the same as those which appear in the previous period, although there was an intensification in the introduction of colonial products from the Gulf of Lyon, grey monochrome ceramics made in the Marseilles workshops, imitated by the indigenous craftsmen, decorated or pseudo-Ionic vases with a light coloured slip, from Marseilles and Empúries, as well as Amphorae, also from Marseilles. After 535 BC Attic vases began to be introduced, with black figures and black varnish, and in the first half of the 5th century BC, the first vases decorated with red figures, although only in small quantities. There are many amphorae from Phoenicia, as well as some from Etruria.

The development of living conditions more favourable for man led to a significant demographic increase with many settlements being established in this period. The priority given to defence, shown by the choice of hilltop sites, implies that this was a time of frequent warfare, although this cannot be confirmed in the Empordà area, with the result that the construction of ramparts has also been interpreted as a symbol of the prestige of the community. During this period, the Indiketa area produced a significant agricultural surplus, particularly cereals, as demonstrated by the existence of large silo fields, both inside and outside the settlements, which were the basis of the intensive trading with the colonial world, which in turn is demonstrated by the introduction of objects, particularly ceramics, originating from different parts of the Mediterranean. In this period a Greek colony was founded in the Gulf of Roses, *Rhodes*, which appears to have been established in the second half of the 5th century BC. On the panel we can see photographs of the *Neapolis of Emporion* and the so-called Hellenistic quarter of Roses, an extension of the colony undertaken in the 3rd century BC. The Middle Iberian Period rampart of Puig de Sant Andreu, and the silo fields found at Puig, inside the settlement, as well as an extensive silo field found outside the site of Sant Julià de Ramis in 1992.

Among the indigenous materials unearthed, as in the previous period, we find both handmade ceramics and those made using the potter's wheel. A good many of the handmade jars have an S shaped profile, with a flat base, and the ornamentation is usually achieved by the application of ridges to the base of the neck. Also highly characteristic of this period, between 450 and 350 BC, are bowls with perforated handles, and large oval jars, without necks, with four handles round their waists, and with their upper parts decorated with combed patterns. Indigenous ceramic production using the potter's wheel during this period offered great variation. From the second half of the 5th century BC onwards the production of painted Iberian pottery, so typical of the previous period, was abandoned and progressively

The Middle Iberian Period: 450-200 BC

Handmade ceramic jar, 425-375 BC.

Ceramic plate made with a light coloured and decorated slip, from an Ullastret workshop, 425-375 BC.

Kylix with a printed decoration and garlanded with ivy leaves.

Urn with handles. Beginnings of the 4th century.

Lekanis with red figures. Style of the Baño painter, 430-420 BC.

replaced by a new production of darker vases with thin walls, of very high quality, which were adorned with white painted motifs, applied after the firing of the vase; this has resulted in their poor condition. The motifs are geometric or representative of plants, frequently copying those which were painted in white onto the Attic vases, particularly in the *Saint-Valentin* style. Other important production included ceramics made with light coloured decorated slip, and dishes from the Catalan coast, known as *Emporitana*. The former were used in the making of vertical lipped plates, decorated with ferules, radial bases or garlanded with olive branches. The latter were highly successful, and continued well into Roman times. The most common shapes for these products were the biconical vases and dishes with the outer edges turned inwards, although numerous examples have been found of imitations of the forms of Attic vases: *skyphos*, *olpes*, *askos*, *kylix*, etc., and later on the forms of Campanian pottery were copied. A great deal of common pottery articles and indigenous amphorae were also found. Towards the end of the

Vase decorated with white paint, showing a rider and horses, from around 400 BC.

period typical painted Iberian pottery was also reintroduced, in the form of the *kalathos*.

In the metal display case there is a variety of metal objects, particularly bronze, surgical instruments and personal decorative items, clasps and pins for securing clothing, rings, earrings, necklaces, etc. along with some iron implements.

Among the imported ceramics the two most numerous groups continue to be Greek and Carthaginian. The Greek material which arrived in greater quantities after the middle of the 5th century BC until the year 350 was Attic pottery, decorated with red figures and with a black varnish, which has been found in all of the houses from this period. Vessels were introduced later with black figures and of poor quality. From among the pottery with red figures there is a great abundance of those in the *Saint-Valentin* style, which only featured geometric or plant designs which were later over-painted in white. Greek amphorae were also found alongside these pieces, almost all of which came from Marseilles. From among the Carthaginian materials, the most common finds have been of amphorae, from Ibiza in the central Mediterranean area, or from the region of the straits of Gibraltar, arriving through the trade links of these centres with neighbouring Empúries, from where they were again redistributed. There are also jars made with the same slip as the Carthaginian-Ibizan amphorae, as well as Carthaginian *olpes,* in increasing amounts towards the end of the period. At the end of the 4th century BC Greco-Italic amphorae began to be introduced, and pottery with a black varnish from the "*petites estampilles*" workshop. The black varnished pottery which predominates all over the Ullastret site during the 3th century BC, were manufactured at the colony of *Rhodes*. In the last decades of this century Campanian ceramics were introduced. Another important product, of evidently Carthaginian origins, are the pots and other cooking vessels with a concave base which were used with a triangular iron support, the use of which indicates the introduction of new cooking methods and new foods for the native population.

Biconical ceramic vase from the Catalan coast IVth-IInd century.

The Late Iberian, or Ibero-Roman, period. After 200 BC

This period represents the progressive transformation of indigenous life through the adoption of the new systems of occupation and exploitation of the land imposed by the Romans. At Ullastret it only lasted a very short time. With the repression of Cato in 195 BC, in the wake of the indigenous revolt, it is possible that some kind of residual occupation of the hill site continued, although this must also have come to an end in the second half of the 2nd century BC, as only the older forms of Campanian pottery have been found. The temple area must have continued in use, as in his area High-Imperial Roman coins have been found. On the panel we can see photographs of urbanised areas in the later stages of the life of the settlements, the colonnaded building of the south-western quarter of Puig and various constructions attached to the southern wall of the Illa.

The display cases exhibit indigenous and imported materials from the period of the later occupation of the settlement, which are the same as the ones corresponding to the final stages of the previous period. There is quite a strong case that the scarcity of clasps found during this period indicates changes of dress style, as the adoption of concave based pots indicates changes of diet.

Trade

Ullastret engaged in barter trade with the Mediterranean colonial world through Empúries, although products from the Celtic world were also introduced, albeit in smaller numbers. There was also trade with inland regions, the aim of which must have been to transport products from the interior to the coast and which must have been engaged in by settlements in several different areas. The panel shows a map indicating the main areas from which Mediterranean imports came. There is also a diagram indicating the marks found on the various types of amphora which have been found at Ullastret. The marks indicated who manufactured the amphorae, where they came from or the ownership of the piece, and where they were made by stamping the clay before firing.

The display cases exhibit various of the different types of amphora found at Ullastret: Carthaginian, from Marseilles, Greco-Italic and Iberian. You can also see fragments of amphorae with their marks, small luxury objects, of multi-coloured Carthaginian slip, miniature amphorae for perfumes, strings of beads, etc. and blue or transparent Celtic glazed; necklace beads, bracelets, etc. Finally there is an exhibition of fragments of the ceramic light coloured slip painted plates manufactured at Ullastret, and which have been found in various Indiketa "*oppida*" from the Empordà coast to the environs of the city of Gerona.

Coinage

Coinage was introduced to the north-western Mediterranean by the Greeks. The first coins to be struck in Catalonia were divisors (obolus) from Empúries, minted during the 4th century BC, and at the end of this century, or the beginning of the next, Empúries and Roses began to strike drachmas. Very few coins have been found at Ullastret, as the site was virtually abandoned at the start of the 2nd century BC, at which time the circulation of money was relatively restricted among the Iberian settlements. The map on the panel shows the origin of the different coins found at Ullastret.

The first display case contains an exhibit of coins from the two Greek colonies in the Empordà, an Empúries obolus from the 4th century BC, and two drachmas, one from Roses and the other from Empúries, from the beginning of the 3rd century BC. In the other display case there are bronze Carthaginian coins, from Carthage and Ibiza, and a Hispano-Carthaginian shekel from the 3rd century BC, bronze coins from Empúries, bearing the inscription "*UNTIKESKEN i EMPORIAE*", bronze Iberian coins from Kese (Tarragona), Arse (Sagunt) and a denari from Bolskan (Osca), an uncial as from the Rome of the last third of the 3rd century BC, and another from the 2nd century BC, as well as ases from the reign of Claudius (41-54 A.D.). This material is testimony to the presence of the first striking of Greek coinage in the Empordà, to the arrival of coinage from both of the opposing sides during the Second Punic War, and to the frequenting of the location after its abandonment as an "oppidum".

Spiritual life.
Beliefs.
The cult of skulls.

The spiritual life of proto-historical communities is one of the most difficult aspects to discover, although the excavation at Ullastret have thrown some light on this matter. At an early stage the temples, at the top of Puig de Sant Andreu, were discovered, one of which is associated with various ex-votive offerings, represented by faces, although it is impossible to know which gods were worshipped here. Leaving aside the representations of gods or mythological personages which appeared on the coins, the only known representations of gods at Ullastret are the *timateria*, with a bust of Demeter, and the terracotta figure of the god Bes. The occasional discoveries of deer antlers imply the cult of Artemis, a goddess who was worshipped at Empúries. As well as these elements which were acquired from the Mediterranean colonial world, the evident existence of the cult of skulls has been demonstrated at Ullastret, the parallels for which appear to be closer to neighbouring southern Gaul. Recently in the Illa d'en Reixac settlement, during the excavation of a large ritual building, remains were discovered which demonstrate the practice of these rites. The trans-Pyrenean influence is also shown by the finds of fire-dogs, which decorated

Human skulls from Illa d'en Reixac, and a group of handmade pots, for ritual use.

the ends of the altar-hearths. Other testimonies to the spiritual life are the animal foundation offerings which have been found under floors or near hearths. At Ullastret the graves of new-born babies have also been found near an altar-hearth in Puig de Sant Andreu. The ritual sacrifice of infants was a habitual practice in the Phoenician world which was also practised by the Iberians.

Firedog from a ritual hearth, in the form of a muzzled head.

On the spiritual life panel you can see a plan of Puig de Sant Andreu, with the location of the temples, a drawing of an idealised reconstruction of one of these, a photograph of the floor plan of the ritual building at Illa d'en Reixac and a coin featuring the god Bes. In the display cases some *ex-votive* offerings are exhibited, along with *timateria* with a bust of Demeter, two terracotta figures representing the god Bes, terracotta fire-dogs in the form of a muzzle, and pottery with an artistic decoration of faces, which in the south-eastern Iberian world are often found in ritual cult locations.

The cult of the skulls panel is illustrated with the floor plan of the ritual building at Illa, and a plan of the northern part of Puig de Sant Andreu, with the location of a silo in which interlocked skulls were found. In the display cases two sets of skulls are exhibited, one from Illa d'en Reixac, accompanied by a set of ceramics which must have been used for ritual practices. One of the skulls shows signs of trepanning. The other set comes from the above mentioned silo at Puig de Sant Andreu, the interlocked skulls were also accompanied by a *La Tène* sword.

The god Bes.

Funerary rites among Iberian communities involved the cremation of human remains at high temperatures, as demonstrated by the colour of the bones which have been found, which later were frequently washed and crushed into small pieces before being put into the cinerary urn and buried. This extreme fragmentation makes it very difficult to identify the sex or the age of the buried individual. Around the urn containing the remains of the deceased, furnishings were placed, offerings and

Spiritual life.
Funerary rites

Pelike with red figures by the Meleagro painter. Beginnings of the 4th century BC.

objects for personal use. The only examples of other kinds of burial are those of new-born babies, or those only a few months old, who were interred inside the houses, or in specially prepared places, as shown in the drawing and photograph which illustrate this panel.

Burials at the necropolis of Puig de Serra were very straightforward, as explained above. One of the display cases exhibits a reconstruction of a more complex grave, the only one that has been found. This was a more or less rectangular cavity cut out of the natural rock and subsequently lined with lime mortar. In an other display case we can see the furnishings from four burials. It has been observed that the urn containing the ashes of the deceased is often an Attic ceramic vase, decorated with red figures, or without any decoration at all, and covered with a black varnish. No warrior's tombs have been found in the necropolis at Serra, and weapons have only been found in one burial from the 3rd century BC, and these are throwing weapons which might well have been used for hunting.

Room 2

Urbanisation and Architecture

Room 2 is dedicated to a specific exhibition of these themes, which have already been explained in the chapter concerning visiting the site. The panels are illustrated with photographs and drawings to which references are made. There is an aerial photograph of the Illa d'en Reixac settlement which shows a type of urban distribution which is far more regular than that of Puig de Sant Andreu, due to the much gentler slopes of the hill on which Illa is located. To one side of the photograph you can see the outline of the southern rampart. In another photograph is one of the corners of this rampart from the middle Iberian Period of Puig de Sant Andreu, to the north of gate 1. A third photograph shows a frontal view of the great wall along the eastern flank of Illa, believed to be a rampart from the early Iberian Period, with a foundation of regular rectangular stones and an adobe elevation forming extremely regular lines. It appears that this section of the wall was, at some time, restored and that the other sections of the wall preserve the stone foundations up to a much greater height.

The panels also illustrate an idealised reconstruction of a group of three terraced houses, each with only one single room, from Illa d'en Reixac. At the back of one of these houses there is a bench which runs along the back wall and the start of the two side walls. All of them have earthenware hearths. You can also see a photograph of one of these houses, which belong to the 4th century, at the time of its excavation. The illustrations are completed with a photograph and a drawing of the floor plan of the temple which is found in front of the museum, a photograph of the western section of the Puig de Sant Andreu rampart, and those of the two cisterns which are currently visible at Puig.

In the room various worked stone exhibits are on view, some of which form part of buildings are, of structural use, bases and capitals, others of decorative use, such as the pieces with rollers and other motifs which decorated the temples. There is also an ashlar from the rampart, which

Detail view of the rampart of what was possibly an early Iberian wall, with stone foundations and adobe elevation. Illa d'en Reixac.

preserves the Iberian lettering which was engraved into it. Finally you can see a kerbstone and a cistern.

Room 3

Language and script

Iberian script, which came into being in the south-east of the Peninsula during the 6th century BC, was the first peninsular native writing system. It combined alphabetical signs and syllabics which while being copied, in mainly from the Greek and Phoenician alphabets, had different phonetic values. It was used from Andalusia to Erau in France. It can be described but it has not proved possible to translate it.

The writing at Ullastret is well documented, particularly in relation to the 4th century BC, as many of the examples of Attic style vessels from this period have inscriptions engraved on them, although it is also found on other objects dated to earlier times, such as on a monochrome grey ceramic *askos*, in the form of a wild animal, or later on various ceramic vessels of the Catalan coast, on Campanian, and other types, and various rolled-up lead sheets bearing inscriptions have also been found. Some of these materials are exhibited,

Askos in monochrome grey ceramic with an Iberian inscription.

Lead sheet with Iberian inscription.

along with coins bearing inscriptions in other languages which have been encountered from various times throughout the Iberian Period, in Greek, Phoenician and Latin. The panel contains drawings of the inscriptions from some of the lead sheets found at Ullastret, and has an Iberian alphabet, with the different variations employed of each of its signs, along with a present day phonetic equivalent.

The economy
Agriculture

Agriculture was the essential economic activity of the Iberians. The Empordà was one of the areas considered to be an important producer of cereals in ancient times. The carbonised remains of agricultural products, and the implements which have been preserved indicate the existence of a well developed agriculture, particularly in terms of dry farming, with ploughs drawn by animal power, but there was also irrigation, as demonstrated by the finds of hoes. On the panels you can see representations of the most important plant species cultivated at that time in Ullastret: hulled barley, naked wheat, emmer wheat and millet, among the cereals, and lentils, peas and beans among the legumes. There are also cultivated vines and, to a lesser extent, olives, a species which was introduced in the Iberian Period. On the panel you can see the representation of a man with a ploughshare, and various implements fixed to handles. In the display case some of the iron implements used in agriculture are exhibited: a ploughshare, hoe, sickle, etc.

The grain was stored in silos, inside which there was an atmosphere which allowed them to be preserved, without germination, for long periods of time. The panel shows the process employed for the excavation of a silo, its use and abandonment. Jars were used for transporting the grain, sacks were probably also used though no remains of these have been found, although needles have been found which are exactly the same as those which are used to sew sacks in modern times. In the display cases there are exhibits of various receptacles used for the storage or transporting of grain, as well as two mills, one of the older type, known as to-and-fro mills, which originated in the Neolithic Period, and another rotary-type mill, which was known in the Iberian settlements in this region from the 4th century BC onwards. There is also a diagram illustrating how rotary mills worked.

Husbandry

This was the second most important economic activity, making a considerable contribution to the Iberian diet, as well as providing raw materials, such as wool, skins and bones which were used to manufacture toiletry implements, decorative objects, knife handles, etc. On the panel there is an illustration of the different domestic species found during excavation work: firstly ovine species, followed by porcine, and to a lesser extent bovine, equine and canine. The bone remains of these domesticated animals is exhibited in the display cases, along with small objects manufactured from bone and horn.

Hunting, fishing and harvesting

These were secondary economic activities, although they are also well documented. The animals hunted were deer, wild boar and rabbit. From the deer only the antlers have been found, although it is possible that they were hunted far from the settlements, and that only the antlers were brought back. These species are shown on the panel, and the display case exhibits throwing weapons which may have been used for hunting. Evidence of fishing activities is shown by finds of bronze fish hooks and net weights, of which some are on display, as well as fish bones which have allowed for the documenting of the species found at the sites, including anguillidae and sparidae, which are also illustrated on the panel. Gathering wild fruits and plants was also practised, as well as sea and fresh water molluscs. In the display case valves from molluscs, found during the excavations, are exhibited.

Craftsmanship

The Iberian socio-economic structure allowed for the emergence of a social class of craftsmen who worked for the community. Among the activities they engaged in the most important were metal-working, pottery, textiles and stone-working.

Metal-working

The main development in this period was the discovery of iron working by the indigenous population. This was accompanied by documentation of the metal working from earlier periods including bronze, lead and silver. The origins of the minerals which were worked can be seen on a map of the region, showing that the main sources were the mountainous areas of Gavarres and the Begur massif, as well as the Pyrenees. There is also a diagram of the operation of a bronze forge, discovered at Illa, and its location at the site. In the display cases there are exhibits of objects manufactured using various metals and found in the two settlements and at the necropolis. In the Iberian Period iron became the metal which was used for all agricultural and craftsman's tools, nails for construction work and the great majority of weapons, swords, spear tips, daggers, etc. Bronze was reserved for the manufacture of toiletry and ornamental implements, jewellery, surgical instruments, small tools with hooks, arrow heads, etc.

The display case exhibits two "La Tène" type swords, which in both cases still preserve the scabbards in which they were kept. At Ullastret only a fragment of a type of sword called a "falceta" has been found; this was by far the more characteristic Iberian weapon, while "La Tène" belonged to the Celtic world.

Textile working

Textiles were made with wool and vegetable fibres (flax and esparto). The looms used were of the vertical type, although only the weights have survived. Ceramic spindle weights have also been found, which were hung from the end of the yarn to twist it. This subject is illustrated by the representation of a woman spinning and a vertical loom. In the display case you can see loom and spindle weights.

Stone-working

The importance of public building works, ramparts, temples, cisterns, and large scale terracing projects, demonstrates the existence of teams of stone-cutters who worked for the community. At Ullastret the quarries used for the construction of the walls have been located, as shown on the map which accompanies the panel. Stones were also gathered together from various sources, some washed down by the rivers, which were also used for various purposes The selective use of different types of stone for different purposes has been well documented. A diagram shows operations for the extraction of stone in the open air.

In the display case we can see various objects from daily life manufactured in stone.

Essential
bibliography

AMICS DE L'ART VELL 1935, Poblat ibèric d'Ullastret, *Memòria de l'obra realitzada des de la seva fundació 1929-1935*, Barcelona, 54-55.

GRACIA, F., MUNILLA, G., RIART, O., GARCIA, O. 2000, *El llibre dels ibers. Viatge il.lustrat a la cultura ibèrica*, Signament edicions i edicions El Mèdol, Barcelona.

MALUQUER DE MOTES, J. 1974, Cerámica de Saint-Valentin en Ullastret (Gerona), *Miscelánea Arqueológica* 1, Barcelona, 411-437.

MALUQUER DE MOTES, J., OLIVA, M. 1965, Hallazgo de dracmas y divisores ampuritanos en las excavaciones de Ullastret, en 1964, *Pyrenae* 1, Barcelona, 85-123.

MALUQUER DE MOTES, J., OLIVA, M. 1965, El nuevo plomo ibérico de Ullastret, *Pyrenae* 1, Barcelona, 124-127.

MALUQUER DE MOTES, J., PICAZO, M., MARTIN, A. 1984, *Corpus Vasorum Antiquorum. Espagne. Musée Monographique d'Ullastret*, Barcelona.

MALUQUER, J., PICAZO, M. 1992, Una casa de final del s.VaC a l'"oppidum" d'Ullastret *Fonaments* 8, Barcelona, 25-51.

MARTIN, A. 1978, La ceràmica decorada amb pintura blanca als poblats indígenes del NE de Catalunya, *Cypsela* 2, Girona, 145-160.

MARTIN, A. 1977, *Ullastret. Guia de les excavacions i el seu museu.*, Girona.

MARTIN, A. 1985, *Ullastret. Poblat ibèric*, Barcelona.

MARTIN, A. 1990, El s.III aC a Ullastret (Baix Empordà). Excavació del Tall LI-1. *8è Col.loqui Internacional d'Arqueologia de Puigcerdà. La romanització del Pirineu.* Puigcerdà, 35-41.

MARTIN, A. 1994, Formació i desenvolupament de la cultura ibèrica a la zona del nord-est de Catalunya. *X Col.loqui Internacional d'Arqueologia de Puigcerdà. Cultures i medi de la prehistòria a l'edat mitjana*, Puigcerdà, 423-434.

MARTIN, A. 1997, *Guies del Museu d'Arqueologia de Catalunya. Ullastret*, Girona.

MARTIN, A., BUXÓ, R., LÓPEZ, J., MATARÓ, M. 1999, *Excavacions arqueològiques a l'Illa d'en Reixac (1987-1992)*, Monografies d'Ullastret, 1, Girona.

MARTIN, A., GENIS, M.T. 1993, Els jaciments ibèrics del Puig de Serra (Serra de Daró). Segles VI-IV aC, *Estudis del Baix Empordà* 12, Sant Feliu de Guíxols, 5-48.

MARTIN, A., SANMARTÍ, E. 1976-78, Aportación de las excavaciones de la "Illa d'en Reixac" al conocimiento del fenómeno de la iberización en el norte de Cataluña a *Simposi Internacional els Orígens del Món Ibèric Empúries 38-40*, Barcelona, 431-447.

MATAS, J. 1986, *Els estanys eixuts* . *Quaderns de la Revista de Girona* 7 .

OLIVA, M. 1953 a 1963, Resultats de les campanyes d'excavació anuals, publicats a *Anales del Instituto de Estudios Gerundenses* , VIII-XVI, Girona.

OLIVA, M. 1962, *Ullastret. Guia de las excavaciones y su museo*, Girona.

OLIVA, M. 1962, Las fortificaciones de la ciudad prerromana de Ullastret. Ensayo de cronologia *Atti del VI Congresso Internazionale delle Scienze Preistoriche e Protostoriche*. Roma, 23-28.

OLIVA, M. 1965, Recintos fortificados de tipo "ciclópeo" en tierras gerundenses *Arquitectura Megalítica y Ciclópea Catalano-Balear*. Barcelona, 89-109.

OLIVA, M. 1967, El nuevo plomo con inscripción ibérica hallado en Ullastret, *Pyrenae* 3, Barcelona, 107-122.

OLIVA, M. 1970, *Ullastret. Guia de las excavaciones y su museo*. 3a.ed.ampliada. Girona.

PICAZO, M. 1977, *La cerámica ática de Ullastret.*. Barcelona.

PONS, E. 1984 , *L'Empordà de l'edat del bronze a l'edat del ferro* . Sèrie Monogràfica del SIAG, 4, Girona.

PUIG i CADAFALCH, J., MARTORELL, F. 1936, Memòria de la Secció Històrico-Arqueològica de l'I.E.C. *Anuari de l'Institut d'Estudis Catalans* VIII (1927-1931) Barcelona, XXIII.

ROVIRA, C. 1992, Recursos minerals i producció metal.lúrgica a l'Empordà durant la protohistòria, *Annals de l'Institut d'Estudis Empordanesos* 25, Figueres, 309-328.

ROVIRA, C. 1993, Estudi arqueometal.lúrgic de l'Illa d'en Reixac, *Revista d'Arqueologia de Ponent* 3 Lleida, 65-149.

SERRA RÀFOLS, J de C. 1945-46, El poblado indiketa de Ullastret, *Empúries* VII-VIII, 359-365.

Additional information

Museu d'Arqueologia de Catalunya-Ullastret

(The Archaeological Museum of Catalonia-Ullastret)
Afores s/n
Puig de Sant Andreu
17114 Ullastret
Tél. 972 17 90 58
Fax 972 17 90 58
http : www.mac.es
e-mail : ullastret@mac.es

Opening times of the site and museum
From 1st October to 31st May
Tuesdays to Sundays from 10am to 2pm and from 3pm to 6pm
Closed on Mondays

From the 1st of June to the 30th of September
Tuesdays to Sundays from 10h to 8h

At Easter, Summer opening times will be observed
Easter Monday open
Closed on 1st and 6th January and on 25th and 26th December

Oficina d'Informació i Difusió, Informació, contractació i reserves (Information and publicity Office, information, bookings and reservations)

Museu d'Arqueologia de Catalunya-Barcelona
Passeig de Santa Madrona, 39
08038 Barcelona
tel: 93 424 65 77/ 93 423 21 49
Fax: 93 424 56 30

Places of interest in the vicinity
Ullastret (1 km) The present day village of Ullastret. Of Mediaeval origin, the village has an important 12th Century wall and a well conserved Romanesque church.
La Bisbal (6 kms) A town of Mediaeval origin with a Mediaeval castle which currently houses the county archives.
Pals (11 kms) An interesting Mediaeval complex with good views over the plain.
Torroella de Montgri (6 kms) Village of Mediaeval origin featuring an arcaded Town Hall square. The Montgrí and Baix Ter museum.

Sant Miquel de Cruïlles (12 kms) Village of Mediaeval origin. The village preserves some important remains.

Peratallada (6 kms) Village of Mediaeval origin with important remains of wall and castle.

L'Escala (21 kms) The Greek and Roman town of Empúries and museum.

Girona (32 kms) Cathedral, Sant Pere de Galligans church, with the Museu d'Arqueologia de Catalunya-Girona (The Archaeological Museum). The Arabian Baths.

How to get to Ullastret

By car:

Motorway A-7 – Barcelona-La Jonquera (Exits Girona Nord or L'Escala-Empúries) then:

N-11 road, Barcelona-La Jonquera

Road, Girona-La Bisbal

Road, La Pera-Serra de Daró

Road, Serra de Daró-Ullastret

© **Text**
Aurora Martin i Ortega

© **Photography and illustrations**
From the institutions and people specified.

Photographic archives MAC-Ullastret
Jordi S Carrera
Oriol Clavell
Mercè Ferré
Francesc Riuró
Pere Rovira
Servei d'Arqueologia. Departament de Cultura de la Generalitat

© **Published by**
Museu d'Arqueologia de Catalunya

Printing
Gràfiques Alzamora, S.A.

Editorial Coordination
Teresa Carreras

In accordance with graphic project by
Josep M. Mir
Contributions: Marta Bachs and Jaume Sellarés

Dipòsit legal: GI-1.307-2001
ISBN: 84-393-5595-5

First edition: December 2001